CAN'T
IS NOT AN
OPTION

Gudrun Lindberg

Can't Is Not An Option

iUniverse books may be ordered through booksellers or by contacting:

iUniverse
1663 Liberty Drive
Bloomington, IN 47403
www.iuniverse.com
1-800-Authors (1-800-288-4677)

ISBN: 978-1-6632-0416-5 (sc)
ISBN: 978-1-6632-0417-2 (e)

Library of Congress Control Number: 2020912140

Print information available on the last page.

iUniverse rev. date: 07/08/2020

One day, I told myself, I will write Renee's story. I will tell of her struggles with dyslexia. I will show her determination to work through it and with it and around it. I will show my determination to do what others said we couldn't... to help her overcome a significant learning disorder and raise a very successful child. This is the Schmidt family story. It is the story of how we became extraordinary.

I am from Sweden and a bit of a rebel. I had moved to the United States to seek fun and fortune when I was just 24. I had left behind a mom and a trio of sisters who thought I was crazy, who said I should stay put and who have missed me ever since, and I've been away about 40 years now.

But I had met Ron in 1966 and had fallen in love. We married and I thought I could never be happier. Then along came Renee, a firstborn, a daughter, and I was even more happy if that's possible. I could hardly contain my joy. Life was good. And it would have remained happy ever after… if this were a fairy tale, but it isn't.

And so my story begins when Renee is born in 1970, a perfectly beautiful child growing blonder by the summers and mixing her first words with my flipflop of Swedish and English with a delight of babytalk.

David was born 6 years later.

Pretty Children.

Handsome husband.

The fairy tale was still in full swing. We bought our first in upscale Clarence, New York. Renee would be starting kindergarten soon. She had already been to pre-school and loved it. Kindergarten should be a piece of cake and it was.

And then she turned six.

First Grade.

The year was 1976. Schools were beginning to hire psychologists. Psychologists were beginning to name disorders. ADD. ADHD. Dyslexia.

At the end of Renee's first semester, I was called into the school social worker's office. I thought it was routine. I thought I'd be hearing accolades about my first born.

"Dyslexia," the social worker intoned. "Your child won't probably graduate from high school," she continued. "We're sure she can't learn another language, certainly never speak one, or even learn to play an instrument, but, Mrs. Schmidt," she went on, "there are jobs for people like your Renee. She will find a place in society."

I felt as if I was bolted to the social worker's chair. "Won't" and "Can't" were the only words I heard in that meeting. The fire in me began.

"Nobody," I thought to myself, "nobody can tell me what my daughter can or cannot do." I unglued myself from the social worker's chair. "We'll see," I said as I pulled opened the office door.

That was the day, the very moment, the Schmidt family became extraordinary, as extraordinary as every family becomes who figures out how to have their child succeed in an educational system that dyslexia,

n., a developmental disorder resulting from the inability to process graphic symbols. Symptoms are difficulty determining the idea content of a simple sentence, difficulty learning to recognize written words, difficulty rhyming; may occur in combination with writing or arithmetic learning problems.

Dyslexia. The Schmidt family now had a cause that would consume them for the next 13 years. It would try their patience, wear them out, change the family dynamics but eventually prove that CAN'T and WON'T are mere words, not destinies.

Dyslexia, I vowed, was not about to
steal my daughter's future.

We soon learned that 20% of the population has some
form of dyslexia and that doctors don't know for sure
what causes it. They believe there is a correlation
between left handedness and the learning disability
in many families. People with dyslexia can and do
learn but the pace differs. Nor does dyslexia limit
success. The International Dyslexic Association
points out famous people with the disorder; George
Washington, Albert Einstein, Alexander Graham
Bell, George Patton, Leonardo DaVinci. Thomas
Edison, Hans Christian Anderson, Whoopi Goldbery
and Tom Cruise. And also the Swedish King.

Renee and I are working together to develop good work habits and an attitude of caring. If successful, this should help to improve reading, math, etc.

It has been a pleasure to have worked with Renee.

Renee appears to be more relaxed and happier about her school work JM 4/78.

Renee is a sweet little girl, I have enjoyed her. JM. 6/78

PARENT COMMENTS

PARENT SIGNATURE

10 Weeks _Gudrun B. Schmidt_

20 Weeks _Ron D. Schmidt_

30 Weeks _Gudrun B. Schmidt_

Room Assignment Next Year _____

ATTENDANCE

	20 Weeks	40 Weeks
Days Absent	1	3
Days Tardy	—	—

Additional help is being provided for Renee in all the subjects. Please continue to encourage daily practice in math and reading.

Renee has shown progress since last marking period. I am pleased with her efforts.

Nice work Renee. ☺

Renee, you have worked very hard this year. Please continue to read this

PARENT COMMENTS

summer and work on your maths. Have a great time in Sweden. ☺ I have enjoyed having you in class.

PARENT SIGNATURE

10 Weeks	Mrs. Ron D. Schmidt
20 Weeks	Gudrun B. Schmidt
30 Weeks	Mr. Ron D. Schmidt
Room Assignment Next Year	Rm. 16 Mrs. Carle

ATTENDANCE

	20 Weeks	40 Weeks
Days Absent	3	6
Days Tardy	1	2

1/11/80

Although at first I was angered by the social worker's blunt diagnosis that fateful day in 1979, I soon learned that early assessment is what saved Renee's future. The fact has been borne out that if educators can make the diagnosis by the first grade, appropriate instruction can begin.

Even though there wasn't much appropriate instruction for dyslexic people in the 1970's, I knew two things I would do for my daughter. I based it on that social worker's doomsday prediction: that Renee would never learn a second language, certainly never speak one, and never learn to play an instrument. Renee didn't know it then, but she was about to learn a new language and play an instrument.

That's where we begin.

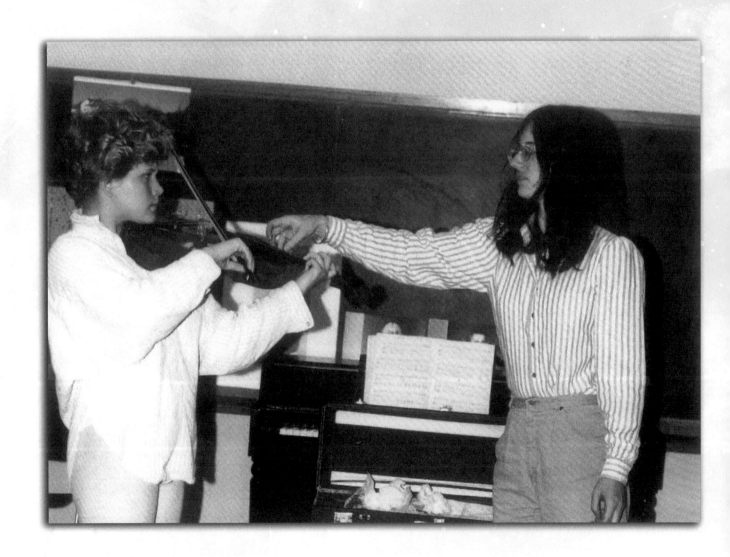

Our journey through the maze of dyslexia began by me contacting people in education. I had Renee tested and retested. State Teacher's college in Buffalo became involved. So we began practicing by reading recipes and cookbooks. We spent four semesters on them. We read. We cooked. We cooked. We read. As Renee began learning to read and comprehend these recipes we both learned to cook. Not a bad result!

Then we met a new friend, Noreen Visone. She had a daughter, Lydia, who played violin. Curious because of the prophecy in that social worker's office, I asked Noreen where her daughter took lessons. She sid Lydia took at Buffalo Suzuki Strings and if Renee was interested I should contact Mary Kay Neal.

Mary Kay set us up with Nancy, one of the teachers at Buffalo Suzuki Strings. Nancy, whose name must mean interminable patience, became Renee's viola teacher.

For the next 12 years Renee became a student of music. Sometimes it wasn't easy. On a number of occasions, renee would have loved to say I CAN'T but since CAN'T is not an option, I often had to pay Renee to play... five dollars a practice session.

And time went on. And as it did Renee actually began to play viola well...better than well... exceptionally.

The Harris Hill school system actually provided many advantages to children with learning disabilities and Renee went to resource classes every day throughout elementary and junior high. We will always be grateful to Mr. Niemes, one of the resource room teachers who taught Renee how to study, how to read, and literally, how to survive junior high. This was no small task.

Music had become her forte as well as her escape. In addition to playing the viola at school functions and then at concerts in the community, she joined the chorale group and began singing her heart out. Music was making a difference in this child's life.

These were the years most children form fast and lasting friendships in school. Not Renee. The Clarence School System had fabulous resource classes for children with learning disabilities and as a result Renee was never in her homeroom long enough to form friendships. In fact, these were the saddest of years. To be kind these were the kids teachers' referred to as the "Bluebirds", you know, the kids who need extra help. But classmates used a different nomenclature, the Dummies.

It broke her heart. "I don't have any friends," she would tell me. Day after day with tears in her eyes she would say, "I'm just one of the dummies."

I sent Renee to Sweden at 13. She was scared. I was scared. Was this such a good idea after all!

In my wildest dreams I never would have thought that a bunch of 10 year fifth graders could break a mother's heart. But they did.

I searched my soul to find a less painful path foe my daughter. And banne mig! I thought of a way. But it would have to wait until Renee was 13, 3 years off. I had to bide my time. It killed me to wait.

To be fair, academically good things happened as Renee progressed from elementary school to junior high. Mr. Niemes, for instance. He was one of the junior high school's resource room teachers and he had good ideas. Renee's grades inched into c's and b's, her reading skills improved, her academic struggles become under her control. She became focused, a talent that would served her well in the years to come.

Soon Renee was 13. It was time to employ my brilliant idea. I had been scheming with my sister, Gunborg, that Renee would skip a year of American school and live abroad in Sweden with Gunborg. She would not be pressured to study academics to the point of tears as she often was in Clarence. Instead she would immerce herself in Swedish culture. Instead she would immerce herself in Swedish culture, study music in Vretstorp near Orebro, learn to ride horseback, become fluent in Swedish and to shake off labels like "dummy."

So at the end of 8th grade I sent my little girl off, alone, to my sister in Sweden. She was scared. So was I. Was this idea of mine so brilliant after all?

This is the little girl
I sent to Sweden.

This was the young woman who returned. In fact, when I picked her at Kennedy, I recognized my luggage before I recognized Renee.

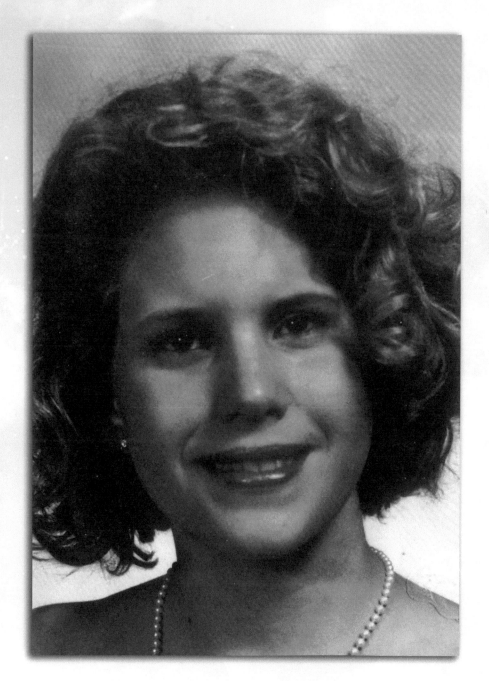

Renee returned from Sweden brimming with poise and confidence and never looked back. She began competing for a seat in the Erie County Youth Orchestra, which she won and stayed with until she graduated. She focused on field hockey and played throughout high school. She took her SATs and matriculated at D'Youville College. She had found her way through the maze of dyslexia.

My daughter continued her studies at Geneseo Community College and discovered her passion and became a physical therapist. She now helps people in their in their own struggle through physical therapy assistant, she found her first job in Virginia. Eventually she was recruited by a firm in New Jersey and this is where we find her now, married to Paul Nusbaumer, happy and successful.

Looking back I wonder how we ever got this point. Was it

a. My will of iron
b. Her will of iron
c. The viola
d. Mr. Niemes resource room
e. My brilliant idea of sending Renee to Sweden for a year, or
f. All of the above

This year Renee turn 40. I think her story is amazing. I'm putting the memories of our extraordinary experience in this little book. When we look upon it we will always remind ourselves that CAN'T IS NOT AN OPTION.

Printed in the United States
By Bookmasters